US AGAINST BREAST CANCER

A Husband's Journal of His Wife's Journey

by Dan Joyce

This book is dedicated to my wife Penny, my children, and all the beautiful souls that supported us during Penny's journey taking on breast cancer.

◆ ◆ ◆

Questions or Freedback?

e-mail: Dan@BiggerBubble.com

◆ ◆ ◆

Copyright © 2019 by Dan Joyce.
All Right Reserved.

No part of this publication may be reproduced, distributed, or transmitted in any form or by any means, including photocopying, recording, or other electronic or mechanical methods, or by any information storage and retrieval system without the prior written permission of the publisher, except in the case of very brief quotations embodied in critical reviews and certain other noncommercial uses permitted by copyright law.

CONTENTS

Title Page	1
Dedication	3
Introduction	7
Chapter 1: Before All This	9
Chapter 2: Finding Out	12
Chapter 3: The First Day of the Rest of Our Lives	16
Chapter 4: Someone is Always Out There	19
Chapter 5: The Next Steps After Surgery	23
Chapter 6: Life Gets More Hectic	26
Chapter 7: Others Have Walked a Mile in Similar Shoes	31
Chapter 8: Surrounded by a Sea of Pink	34
Chapter 9: The First Day of Chemo Treatment	37
Chapter 10: Chemo Takes a Punch Landing Us Back in the Hospital	40
Chapter 11: Hair Today, Gone Tomorrow	44
Chapter 12: Back to the Hospital Again	47
Chapter 13: Getting to the End of the Journey with Appreciation	52
Postscript: Cancer Free!	55

INTRODUCTION

Cancer is a club nobody wants to join, and yet membership is too high. Dealing with the fog of being diagnosed, and the treatment that follows is an intimidating experience. There is a lot of "fear of the unknown." Everyone is different. Every case is different. Prescribed treatments are different. But many aspects of the family journey through breast cancer are similar.

This is the story of my journey supporting my wife who was diagnosed with breast cancer in August 2011.

The government reported that from 2011 to 2015, there were nine hundred and fifteen new breast cancer cases of females under the age of forty-nine in Hennepin County, Minnesota. That averages to less than two hundred new cases a year. My wife Penny was one of them. Penny was thirty-nine years young when she noticed a strange new lump on her left breast. At this time of life, Penny and I had three children – twins. Erin and Braden - five, and daughter Ava - six.

Diagnosis is always the surreal stage for the cancer patient;

it is that point where the patient is in between two worlds – reality and denial. This was our new reality that we needed to take on. This was a fight we would rather have avoided altogether if left to our discretion. Nevertheless, the mountain that was before us was made of cancerous cells and as much as we wanted to run away from the battlefield, we knew it was not a question of flight or fight. There was only one option in it for us. We had to take this battle on against breast cancer.

Armed with good wishes, support from both hospital staff, friends and family, and unbending faith in the power of recovery come what may, Penny began her journey through cancer. On this journey, our family experienced many emotions, most of which were borne by the power of love and support we received from family and our community. Along the way, my wife revealed depths of strengths she never knew were housed inside of her. We experienced the immeasurable deposits of love that people showed her and our entire family. It is true that no successful life is an island and Penny's fight with cancer has taught me that whatever one does in life, you never achieve success alone.

You can say cancer gave Penny more grit. That would be true. But it has also made us become more aware of the daily battle families like ours are winning or losing (unfortunately). Cancer is a disease that once it lands on your doorstep, it changes your life forever. I am Penny's husband, and we lived the challenge. This is a journal of our family journey through the world of breast cancer.

CHAPTER 1: BEFORE ALL THIS

"A life lived in love will never be dull." – Leo Buscaglia

❖ ❖ ❖

In the summer of 1997, a boy from Maine randomly met a girl from Iowa at a waterfront bar in Dewey Beach, Delaware. The band, "Love Seed Momma Jump" had the energy of the crowd high. Fueled by that energy and a few beers, I worked up the courage to introduce myself to a group of attractive girls in their twenties standing by the bar. One person more than others caught my eye and my interest.

"Hi, I'm Penny. I am a traveling nurse from Iowa," she said.

From there we drank and danced the night away, enjoying the time of our lives. At the end of the night, I left her my number and asked that she give me a call. These were the days before everyone had a cell phone. She was a traveling nurse without a permanent phone number. Sunday afternoon as I drove back to Washington, DC. I thought a lot about Penny from Iowa and wished I had some way to follow up with her. It was up to her to connect back.

Thursday the following week Penny called. She was supposed to work her final weekend shift at the hospital. Her co-workers planned a going away party for her. But urged by her girlfriend Angel, she decided to call in sick and head back to Dewey

Beach one last time before she left for Seattle and her next assignment.

At some point of life, you must make that choice of who you want to spend the rest of your life with from the sea of choices. For some, this is quite a daunting task. For me it was an easy choice once I met Penny.

Penny was the one and I didn't need a sage to tell me this was where my heart would plant its' root. Penny was my kind of girl, the type you wanted to take home to meet your family. I was drawn to her wonderful personality, her smile, her spirit, and her overall beauty. There was something wonderfully different and unique about Penny. I knew that this was the woman I wanted to spend the rest of my life with.

My first assignment was to woo Penny since there was obviously chemistry between us. We agreed to stay in touch. After a long drive across the country, she and Angel arrived in Seattle, Washington. We committed to a "bi-coastal" relationship. We spoke on the phone every day for hours. It was a great way to learn more about one another. The marketing maven in me launched an all-out campaign to win her attention with letters, mixtapes, and quirky small gifts. For example, I sent her a little bottle of Tabasco hot sauce with a note saying, "You are hot stuff."

A year later we got engaged on a perfect summer night in Maine and a year after that we got married on September 1999 in Bellevue, Iowa. My career with Honeywell relocated us to Minneapolis, Minnesota. After a roller coaster experience trying to have children, followed by a year of IVF (in vitro fertilization), our first daughter Ava was born to us on Christmas day 2004. She was the best Christmas gift we ever received. Quickly after we were blessed with twins, Braden and Erin on July 3rd, 2006. Our family was complete, and life had begun in earnest.

CHAPTER 2: FINDING OUT

"It takes both rain and sunshine to make a rainbow." - Roy T. Bennett

❖ ❖ ❖

July 15th, 2011 started as a regular warm and sunny summer day. I was in Maine to attend my 25th Portland High School reunion. I was looking forward to enjoying the tastes of Maine while I was in town and catching up on cherished childhood friendships. Penny and the kids were back in Minneapolis. It didn't make sense for them to come back to Maine with me since plans were in place for us to be in Maine for our annual vacation a few weeks later in August. We traveled back to Maine at that time every summer to honor my dad's birthday.

I knew Penny had a biopsy as a follow-up to a doctor's appointment to check on some lumps she recently discovered. The initial thought was that it was a benign condition. The doctor was not overly worried but wanted to send her for an MRI just for added peace of mind. We had concerns but both thought everything would be fine.

Penny called me around two in the afternoon. I knew instantly from the quiver in her voice that the day was going to take a turn in a new direction. My wife was in a ton of emotional pain having just heard her new fate. The results were positive for breast cancer. Two spots in the left breast, three others were benign.

My heart sank.

I felt so far away at a moment when I wanted to be so close. I wanted to reach through the phone and give her a warm, comforting hug. I was dealing with my own shock while simultaneously trying to figure out what was the best response as a husband whose wife just got news that she had cancer. Do I cry it out with her? Tears were easy to come by. Do I stay strong and positive to help minimize the situation? Strength was hard to come by and so we started a conversation filled with a roller coaster of emotions. I started to think a million thoughts searching for answers to unanswerable questions. Why us? What did this all mean? How bad is this? What do I do next?

I wasted no time leaving Maine for Minneapolis. A week went by living in a world of the unknown, thinking the worst, hoping for the best. Penny had some additional tests. We had an appointment to meet with her surgeon, Doctor Margit Bretzke on Friday, July 22nd. It was at that time we would get a better picture of what lay ahead.

The appointment with Penny's surgeon was sobering. I am not sure why, but we were still setting our expectations that things would not be that bad. Sure, she had cancer, but we caught it early. But the news from the doctor was heavier than expected. The initial grade of cancer is rated on a scale of 1 to 3, with 3 being the faster-growing cancer. A higher grade means that a cancer was growing fast and has potential to spread to other parts of the breast or body. Penny's cancer was graded a 3.

The doctor went over the battle plan. It all came at us faster than our minds could absorb or comprehend. I tried to take some notes, but it was challenging to record the words while digesting what it all meant to our lives. It would be a three-stage fight. One, two, three.

One: total mastectomy of the left breast. We hoped for maybe a lumpectomy. Get in and remove the few small cancerous spots. Not so. We were going all the way.

Two: Chemo. Ugh! Not what we wanted to hear. We hoped for basic radiation. As the doctor explained the potential side effects of nausea, fatigue and hair loss, my heart dropped lower.

Three: Herceptin. Herceptin is a miracle drug widely used to treat early-stage breast cancer that has spread to the lymph nodes. Penny would need to get intravenous therapy, aka IV drips of Herceptin for a year which meant many visits to Abbott Hospital.

I remember thinking, "A YEAR!?" My God. I knew how I felt sitting in my chair listening to all that. I could only imagine how my wife was feeling in the chair next to me.

We had vacation plans to Maine August 3rd to the 13th. We asked the doctor if an extra week mattered at this point. Maybe we could enjoy something fun as a family before we headed into the cancer battlefield. The doctor said we should get treatment going right away. We knew summer vacation in Maine was not as important at that point. The doctor left the room, and we started to discuss the news. Tears rolled down our eyes as we tried to process the information. It all came in faster than we could grasp. My prior innocent thinking that this wasn't going to be so bad had been quickly dashed. This was going to be a big impact on our lives.

The next few days were spent absorbing the news and preparing for our life ahead. We started to share the news with loved ones — family, friends, and neighbors. At first, we couldn't share the news with others without an emotional quiver in our voices. The more we told our story, the easier it was to deliver the news. What would easily drive us to tears soon became matter-of-a-fact information. But I knew the pain was still deep inside.

How did Penny get cancer? She never smoked – so it wasn't due to tobacco. She was fit, so it wasn't due to lack of physical activity. Was it something in her diet? Was it linked to birth control pills or recent IVF treatment? Maybe her work as a nurse put her at increased risk. Could it be from the chemical coating in non-stick pans, or too much sunbathing? What did she do wrong and what should she avoid in the future? The truth is we will never know. We just needed to accept she had it and deal with it.

CHAPTER 3: THE FIRST DAY OF THE REST OF OUR LIVES

"Take care of your body. It is the only place you have to live."
–Jim Rohn

◆ ◆ ◆

My wife is my hero. She approached her surgery on August 3rd, with a ton of strength maintaining a positive attitude. I believe a positive attitude is part of the medicine for a successful life.

We headed out for breakfast with the kids and her parents. This would be Penny's final meal before surgery. It was nice to enjoy a bit of innocent normality before taking the first big step: mastectomy surgery.

After talking it over as a couple, Penny decided to go for a double mastectomy. I am sure if I voted otherwise, Penny would still of had a double mastectomy. Her mind was made up. She wanted to remove any future fear of the unknown in the other breast. She wanted to avoid living life with a mismatched chest.

The hours ticked by slowly for me like a man waiting for ketchup to drip out of an almost empty bottle. We left for the hospital at 1:30 pm. Penny was in good spirits as they prepped her for surgery. She maintained that positive, upbeat attitude as her mom; dad and I made chit-chat to distract all of us from the weight of the procedure ahead. We tried to stay off food topics since Penny was hungry from not being able to eat before surgery. For some reason, it is hard to NOT talk about food when you don't want to talk about food.

The nurse came in — time to go.

The wall of emotion that everyone built broke briefly as we said final goodbyes and gave best wishes. We hugged and kissed goodbye, and they wheeled her away to surgery. My wife was about to go under the knife and have part of her body thrown away. The sheer thought of it almost made me topple over. How long before she came out? I wondered. What if they found something worse? This was not the time to allow negative thoughts to take root in my mind. By the time Penny was out, she would need me in the best of spirits to help her get through the next couple of days, weeks, months. There was no telling when this nightmare would go away.

Hours went by as we waited during Penny's surgery to be over.

Finally, the lead surgeon came out to report, "All good news." The surgery went well. They didn't find any additional signs of cancer. We caught it early and got at it quickly. The cancer had not spread to the lymph nodes. Initial tests all came back in our favor. She was in stage one.

Good news is therapeutic; it changes your outlook on life and helps you through a bad day. I think the last time I felt so happy was the birth of my last children. A rush of good feelings poured through my body and mind. I felt guilty feeling so good as others in the waiting area were taking on their own family challenges. But I felt we were due for some good news after all the bad news we had received the past few weeks.

I set about sharing the good news with family and friends who had been extremely supportive of us since we first found out Penny had cancer. It was great to share positive news. We were all in this together. So many wonderful friends have invested themselves in this journey. This time, there was no quiver in the voice; it was easy to report good news.

I feel that the community of well-wishers, good thoughts and prayers played a role in our good fortune after surgery. It was extremely heartwarming to see the outpouring of love from friends and family close and far away. On our journey to recovery, I have come to understand that one of the greatest steps to healing especially when dealing with life-threatening cases is the availability of a strong support group. I don't wish for anyone to go through a bad situation, but I do hope everyone gets to feel the circle of love that neutralizes the stinging pain of a bad situation. In his book, "How to win friends and influence people," Dale Carnegie said: "The greatest need of any individual is the need to feel loved, valued and appreciated." Thanks to a loving circle around us, that need is filled.

If there is a positive of this journey so far, it is witnessing people at their best, rising. At the end of the day, it is the relationships in our lives that matter most and holds the richest value. Penny had the right people around her and as a result, our fight was not alone. We had many in the frontline of the battle against cancer with us.

Our journey is far from over. Penny has weeks of recovery and months of further treatment with chemo and Herceptin. But after yesterday's surgery, we are starting this journey with a good first step. One step at a time, one day at a time...

CHAPTER 4: SOMEONE IS ALWAYS OUT THERE

"Treasure the love you receive above all. It will survive long after your good health has vanished." – Og Mandino

◆ ◆ ◆

As Penny recovered in the hospital, I headed home to help care for our kids. I had a hard time falling asleep the previous night. It wasn't because I was not tired. It was because my bed felt a little uncomfortable without Penny occupying her normal spot next to me. After years of always having her there, it feels uncomfortable when she is not. I have become used to her stealing the covers, taking the good pillows and pushing me to the edge of the bed. I have grown comfortable with all that. It is nice to feel that someone I love is there. I guess we all need a security blanket of some type. Penny was my security blanket of all times.

It has been a more sobering experience for Penny in the hospital. I guess the pain medications were wearing thin. She was more uncomfortable today. Headache, pain, and nausea – she got to experience the patient *trifecta*. It is hard to see someone you love in so much pain.

It seems insurance companies try to push patients out of the hospital faster than it takes to check in. I guess "they" are our friends at the insurance company. Don't get me wrong; I am thankful for having health insurance, but Penny wasn't ready to leave the great 24-hour care of the medical team at Abbott Hospital. Thankfully it was decided that her stay would be extended another night.

The Abbott medical team has some of the warmest and kindest hearts one could find in a hospital environment around these parts. From Penny's doctor to the team of nurses who waited on her, I was thankful we didn't have bad hospital treatment to add to our already tired souls. They took turns checking her IV-line, temperature and general response to treatment. I wondered how we'd cope when we finally left the hospital for our home.

Penny slept most of the day, broken by periodic disruptions by the medical staff doing check-ins and administering what I imagine were some pretty good drugs. I sat in her darkened room for hours, switching chairs periodically to mark the passing of time. I sat there all day because I knew she might be more *uncomfortable* if I wasn't near during the brief periods when she woke up. Based on my experience trying to sleep the night before, I knew how nice it is to feel that your loved one is close by. We all need a security blanket.

We got a call from Penny's lead surgeon later in the day. She reported the results of her detailed biopsy. It was another day of good news. The doctor reported that the three nodes all tested negative and the biopsy on the cancer that had been removed qualified her as a Stage 1a. We caught cancer quite early.

Receiving the news that Penny was a Stage 1a cancer patient was the most perky I'd seen Penny in days. Good news is great medicine. The lower stage will hopefully lessen the intensity of her follow-up chemo and Herceptin treatments. I don't think it makes it go away, but hopefully, it makes it all easier. We will learn the exact details when we meet with her oncologist in a few weeks.

I yawned and scratched my head. It had been a long day. Outside, life continued in a blur. I watch from the small, square window in the door to Penny's room as nurses and doctors alike whizzed by like bees. They were on their way to save another life. I thank them for saving Penny's.

Penny looks beautiful in the hospital gown. Beside her are some flowers from a friend. They complement the sheets that cover her body and I smile at how perfect she looks. I sigh and reach out to touch her head, brushing back a strand of hair. My heart misses a beat. My wife's locks were glorious.

"We are going to beat this thing Penny," I say softly.

She stirs but does not open her eyes. An effect of the drugs coursing through her system perhaps. My mind wanders off to another place. I think back to when we found out Penny was pregnant after many failed attempts. We had welcomed our daughter Ava with so much joy. I never thought I would feel the way I felt the day my first child was born, until Braden and Erin arrived. Over the years, I have watched my wife transform from the woman I met many years ago on that beach in Delaware to a mother to three adorable kids and my greatest support system. I was a blessed man. Everything will be okay.

Over the week, Penny's friends touch base to show support.

Many ask, "how are you? You look good." It sometimes feels uncomfortable and awkward to show support. There is a natural tendency of not wanting to interrupt, intrude or potentially say the wrong thing. But you want to let the person know you care and are thinking about them. It is also hard for the patient who wants to receive support and share, but at times gets tired of telling the same story. Sometimes it is nice to escape the situation. My friend Lynn said her approach is to show up and ask, "Do we want to talk about this, or do you want to talk about other things today?" That approach leaves the option for the patient. Some days are great for health venting, while others are perfect for escaping and pretending life is normal.

There were many people looking for information on how Penny was doing. I started a website to provide updates about

Penny's journey. I investigated Caring Bridge but decided to set up my own website using Weebly.com. I wanted to learn if I could do it and discovered it was easy to do. The website was received with a lot of warmth and we managed to get a considerable followership. The site for Penny was an interesting experience. In an odd way, I think everyone participating in the journey was getting back as much as they gave. We all witnessed the stitching of a warm security blanket by a strong community of family and friends. We can all take comfort knowing that blanket will be there to put around others when they need it. In a way, we are all connected and what affects one, affects everyone else. It is comforting to know we are not alone on this journey of life.

CHAPTER 5: THE NEXT STEPS AFTER SURGERY

"The power of community to create health is far greater than any physician, clinic or hospital." – Mark Hyman

◆ ◆ ◆

Friday morning, I arrived at the hospital, Penny was feeling much better than the day prior. She was still in pain where they cut into her chest, but her spirits were back. She was at a point where she could continue recovery at home. Penny was released from the hospital Friday afternoon at 2pm. We packed up her flowers and cards and headed home.

The next stage had begun.

I remember how cautious I was driving my newborn children home for the first time. I had that same cautious feeling driving Penny home. The roads around Abbott Hospital are not that great. I could feel every bump I went over magnified ten times. I didn't want to add any extra pain to Penny's ride home.

Soon we were home, and we got her into bed. We tried to mimic the wonder of the hospital's Craftmatic Adjustable Bed. We spent time trying to get enough pillows, plumped up and placed best we could to make her somewhat comfortable. After much effort on our part, we managed to get it good enough. Soon she settled back into a deep sleep.

The kids came home from seeing the Carondelet School production of Charlie Brown with their grandma. They were happy to see their mom. Of course, being young kids, they were jumping on the bed and jumping on mom not understanding that mom was fragile. They were not fully aware of the surgical cuts and pain under mom's shirt. I think the joy of seeing the kids masked any temporary added pain. We decided to not make it much of an issue, but gently control the situation. Children notice more than we think they do and sometimes, the impact of pain on them can be long-lasting. We wisely taught the kids the new temporary way to be around mom. I am sure Penny misses the hugs from her kids, but they will be back after she heals.

Sleeping through the night was another task. Penny woke up several times at night and the task of being fully alert fell on me. It reminded me of the first night caring for a restless newborn child. Her pain medicine dose was for every six hours, and she wasn't going to miss her chance to throttle down the pain. Penny's mom, Jane, has been staying here the past days to help us. She is wonderful and has made my job easier. I am pretty sure I have the best mother-in-law in the world. I will be sad to see her go.

The good news is that after Jane leaves, my sister Mary Ellen is coming in from Maine to lend some support. Mary Ellen is the second oldest of my five older sisters. She will tag in for the week to help. Mary Ellen had planned to be on vacation with us while we were in Maine. She looked forward to spending time at my sister Kathy's lake home with her nieces and nephew. Since we canceled our vacation to Maine; she offered to fly to us in Minnesota. We look forward to her visit and the extra set of hands.

We spent the next day receiving lots of cards, phone calls, e-mails, and food. The food rolled in faster than we can eat or find freezer space. It is a good problem. We also received a handful of cards and phone calls from people who are friends of people we know. Often, they have a personal connection of some type fighting breast cancer. The generosity of people's thoughtfulness and spirit has been intense. It is my personal belief that one of the greatest ways to fight sickness is to have ample goodwill and support around you. My wife had more than an ample share of love from those who had cared enough to reach out to us.

As days go on, Penny continues to recover well at home. Every day the healing advances and she is a day closer to having the surgery behind her. The next phase is the chemo. We have plans to meet with Penny's oncologist on Wednesday. We will learn more details of the next phase. Overall, we feel fortunate that we are on a good path to recovery.

CHAPTER 6: LIFE GETS MORE HECTIC

"True friendship is like sound health; the value of it is seldom known until it is lost." – Charles Colton

◆ ◆ ◆

My goodness! What an August week it has been. I am not a professional plate spinner but that is what life feels like of late.

Where do I start?

We had our big milestone appointment with the oncologist on Wednesday. We met Doctor Stuart Bloom. He came highly recommended. He has a wonderful bedside manner. He is great and witty at all the appropriate times. Obviously being married to me; Penny must have a good sense of humor. Dr. Bloom spent over an hour with us going through everything. He made us feel like Penny was his only patient. I never got a sense that our time with him was limited.

There is a security that comes from sensing that one is not being hurried through preliminary hospital proceedings. It helps the patient and their loved one alike deal with the psychological strain and stress of looking forward to a full recovery. Dr. Bloom provided the most detailed account of things. He broke the tension in the most unlikely manner a doctor would ever start a conversation with a patient.

"Shit! You have cancer," he said and then he went on a tangent about how one of his older patients was offended by his use of the word "shit." I am not sure if there was "really" a patient, or if the story was used as a good ice breaker. Either way, it was effective in the moment.

Unlike trying to remember the blur of news from prior doctor visits, he wrote out detailed notes by hand as he discussed things with us. He started out his note, "Darn it – you have breast cancer. The good news is Dr. Bretzke removed all the cancer we know about. But cancer is sneaky. Even before you know it, mere microscopic breast cancer cells can leave the breast and spread to other parts of the body."

Surgery got the cells we know of. Now we go after the potential cancer cells that we don't know about to avoid any chance of cancer coming back in another area of the body. Dr Bloom's role is to help us with the odds.

There are website calculators where doctors can put in variables and get a good feel for the statistical math of cancer – the "odds." In Penny's case, if she had no additional treatment, studies show 70 out of 100 patients with the same variables have no reoccurrence. But, 30 out of 100 patients had some form of residual cancer in the body. With the next Chemotherapy phase, we are working to improve the odds from 70% to 92% in our favor. Right now, 92% is the best we can do – but those are great odds. We can live with 92%.

Penny will start Chemo treatments in four weeks (after Labor Day). She will have to go for IV drips of Taxotere, Carboplatin, and Herceptin once every three weeks for the next eighteen weeks. This will last until the end of the year. Each treatment will last for three to four hours. This will also be the phase where Penny will take on side effects of nausea, fatigue and hair loss. She's likely to be more worn out as the treatment wears on.

Taking on pain seems manageable, but the thought of losing hair seems daunting to Penny. According to the doctor, she will likely lose her hair seventeen days after she starts her treatment.

Women love their hair. Penny's hair has received decades of constant care, a battery of the best hair products, and numerous stylings. Now we must hit the reset button. We are not sure how the kids will react to all this. The nurse told us about a website where they sell dolls that lose their hair to help explain a mommy hair loss to young kids. It will be interesting to see how they react to all this. I think they will take it in stride, without any lasting impact.

This reminded me of a story about Joe George at Honeywell. He was one of our Vice Presidents of Sales. He left Honeywell a few years ago after a long, distinguished career. He is a leader with lots of heart. I remember when he was getting his MBA at the University of Minnesota, he shaved his head bald. Many wondered why he would do that. I later found out there was a woman in his MBA class that was going through chemo and lost her hair. In an act of solidarity and support, her classmates all shaved their heads as well. Maybe Braden and I will get our heads shaved to support mom... heck, maybe Ava & Erin too. We can be the bald Joyce family.

It's just hair; it will grow back.

I think the hard part of hair loss, is the loss of control. Penny and I talked about "owning" this and taking control back. Like having her hair cut short and donating her hair to charity – such as Locks for Love.

The longest days will be from now until the end of the year. After the chemo treatments are completed, Penny will continue Herceptin IVs every three weeks. The good news is Herceptin doesn't have any hard side effects. Herceptin is an antibody to the HER2 molecule. Penny tested HER2 positive, which made her eligible to receive the drug. I guess not everyone is HER2 positive and would benefit. Both Dr. Bloom and Dr. Bretzke stated that being able to receive Herceptin is a wonderful thing. They called it the biggest breakthrough in the battle against breast cancer in the past ten years. The antibody will significantly reduce any chance of spread or reoccurrence.

After surgery, Penny had two drains installed in her chest called Jackson-Pratt (JP) drains – one located on each side of her body. The device suctions and collects fluid from the surgical area. The drain promotes healing and recovery and reduces the chance of infection. The drains are left in place until the drainage slows enough for the body to reabsorb fluid on its own. I have had the fun task of draining them a few times a day and charting the amount of fluid collected. I assume this is another test of the marriage vow I took, "for better or for worse, in sickness and in heath."

The days go by and healing continues.

Penny had her Jackson-Pratt Drains removed a week or so after surgery. She will finish recovering from surgery for the next few weeks, until the Chemo treatment start.

It has been nice having my sister, Aunt Mary Ellen visiting us. She has been a great help with the kids. I will miss her when she leaves on Saturday to go back to Maine.

Taking care of young kids is hectic. Someone always needs something. Someone always wants a different thing to eat or drink. Someone sometimes misses the potty. The dishes and the cloths constantly pile up and need to be washed. And everyone is constantly making a mess of the house moving the destruction from room to room. Your time is not your own when you are taking care of a family and kids. I can't wait to go back to my real day job. I admire housewives.

We had a maid in the past, but Penny decided it was silly as a stay at home mom to have a maid. She could cover things. But I hired back the maid we used in the past, Marta. Now we have one less thing to worry about.

Our house has been a beehive of activity with deliveries from UPS, FED-EX, florists, and the like. The mailman delivers a new pile of cards every day. Great-hearted neighbors and friends have been dropping by with food and treats. Penny has received a stream of visitors. The kids are getting spoiled as wonderful people have provided thoughtful gifts for the kids as well. From our kids view, they are probably thinking this time in life is better than a birthday or Christmas.

We are getting through. We continue one day, one step at a time. The next week is the one I worry about as Aunt Mary Ellen leaves and I head back to work. I hope Penny will be well enough to care for the kids. I am looking into finding some future help with the kids and take stress off Penny.

CHAPTER 7: OTHERS HAVE WALKED A MILE IN SIMILAR SHOES

"Without your health, you've got nothing going on. I thank God every day for good health." –Ric Flair

❖ ❖ ❖

We have joined a club that no one aspires to join, the breast cancer club. Unfortunately, we are discovering that there are many others in this club. There are more than I ever thought before I became hyper-aware of breast cancer. It has been heartwarming how members of this club support one another — the power of numbers and support. We got a letter from a dear family friend, Ann, who captured our experience spot on, she wrote:

"Dear Penny & Dan
First, there's the dreaded wait for biopsy reports followed by the pit-of-the-stomach call that your fears are confirmed.
  Next the blur of appointments and consultations, information and decision making as to the best procedure for you...
  Dates, surgeries, procedures, and recovery follow along with the struggle of healing physically and working at emotional acceptance to mind and body...
  Always the concerns of all family members...
  Then the process of living through the treatments...

But what gets you through is the caring medical staff who become your "lifeguards" and always the ever-present support, caring, love and prayers of family and friends.

Even though it will be more than just tomorrow, one day you will once again feel the light on your heart, the weight of worry and concern will be lifted, and there will be joy of life once again.

In the meantime, I hope the words and message in this card will give you the strength needed each day – and always BELIEVE!!"

We knew she had been on this journey firsthand as a breast cancer survivor. She captured it well.

In another example, we came home one day to a message on our answering machine. A woman indicated in the message that she and Penny had never met before, but she had heard about Penny through common friends in our Carondelet School community. It is a small community.

She went on to share that she is also a young breast cancer survivor that had surgery in April. She reached out to show support and be a friend to talk to – someone that knows how Penny feels because she has recently gone through a similar situation.

Her name is Kim.

Kim called back a few days later and caught us at home. I put her on the phone with Penny, and they chatted for a long while. During the conversation, they discussed how hard it is for breast cancer patients recovering from surgery and with skin stretching plates in their chest to sleep comfortably. It is painful for Penny to sleep flat. Kim said she had a chair that she wanted to pass onto Penny. Penny would be the fourth breast cancer survivor to recover in this chair.

The healing cancer chair allows patients to recline verses sleeping flat which helps alleviate pain after surgery. So instead of *"The Sisterhood of the Traveling Pants,"* this was *"The Breast Cancer Sisterhood of the Traveling Chair."* The chair has provided great comfort for Penny.

As part of Brest Cancer Awareness, WCCO a local news station featured a story about the chair and the special bond of new friends, who face similar situations, supporting one another.

Unfortunately, there will be a next person to pass the chair onto when Penny no longer needs it. Frankly, I cannot wait until we pass it on. It would mean recovery on Penny's part and hope for another like her. We have been privileged to hear firsthand accounts of breast cancer and cancer in general, survivors. Some of these people may never have the chance to share their stories with the world but they eagerly pass it on to people like them still fighting the disease or on their way to recovery. I guess that is the primary purpose of me sharing my story.

CHAPTER 8: SURROUNDED BY A SEA OF PINK

"All the money in the world can't buy you back good health." –Reba McEntire

◆ ◆ ◆

Penny went in for a genetic testing appointment at Abbott Hospital last Friday. They tested her DNA to see if her cancer is nature or nurture. Mostly, genetic testing is done to help others in the bloodline take precaution if it is found in the genetics that there could be a higher risk of getting breast cancer. In our case, Penny wanted to know if our two girls may be at higher risk in life ahead.

Our neighbor, Howard drove Penny and dropped her off as I got the kids ready and out of the door for various play dates and activities. It was a wild morning with people coming and going - the phone ringing, people at the door knocking, kids in chaos, the maid cleaning and myself in the middle trying to keep all the plates spinning. I have become quite adept at managing most of the little domestic chores that arise in the house.

Penny called to let me know she was ready to be picked up from the hospital. On my way to Abbott, I drove around Lake Calhoun. I was met with a beautiful sight. There was a sea of people in pink as far as I could see. The Susan G Komen "3-Day for the Cure" had just begun. Great people walk-run sixty miles over 3-days to raise money for breast cancer research. The first mile was across my path. The timing was wonderful. The massive sight of the sea of pink humanity continues the theme about the power of numbers to take on life challenges. I rolled down my window, honked my horn and waved my hand to show love and support. I probably looked like a lunatic, but in that moment I didn't care. I felt emotional because in a way, the crowd was supporting my wife. The sea of pink was for my wife. I was grateful.

A year ago, I probably would have impatiently snaked my way out of the mass of humanity and passively drove on. But a year ago, Penny did not have breast cancer. Or rather we were unaware of the foreign visitor that potentially had been quietly growing alongside my family. In the moments of our deepest needs, we are forced to understand the pains and worries of people around us.

Penny went wig shopping with two of her girlfriends, Ann and Megan. Penny's youngest brother Justin is getting married in October and Penny is not excited about the fact that she will lose her hair by the wedding. She spent a few hours trying on wigs and was comforted that things won't be that bad. She will look fine in a wig.

Cancer really gets in the way of life. We had plans. Now everything needs to be reevaluated. Penny thought about trying to delay chemo until after her brother's wedding. Then it could be delayed after my trip overseas, or a trip she planned to take to Mexico with girlfriends. Yup, cancer is not a very considerate visitor when it comes to timelines and a calendar of previous plans. We have settled our mind that cancer comes first – we can't delay treatment. We will just have to realign our life around our new reality.

Penny decided to cut her hair short to help the kids manage

the change in her appearance when she loses all her hair. It was also a way for Penny to take control of a situation beyond her control. The shorter hair is a first step, followed by chemo hair loss, a wig, a wrap and whatever else makes my wife feel closer to normal. Penny has been a long-time client of the Chair Hair Salon in Minneapolis. After becoming aware of her situation, the owner of the salon offered Penny a free cut. It was very nice of him. Ongoing acts of kindness lift the soul. Good deeds usually come back in spades. His choosing to run his business with heart makes me feel positive he will have a long, prosperous business.

I found someone to help with the kids while Penny undergoes Chemo treatments. I offered Brianne, my 19-year-old niece from Maine to come and stay with us for six weeks from mid-September through October. She has never visited the mid-west. This is her first plane trip and will be a nice opportunity for her to test ground outside of Maine. I am looking forward to her experiencing mid-west people and life.

This is the last week before the kids go back to school. Summer is ending. Next week we will get the kids into their new school routine. Penny will meet again with her oncologist. We will both attend Chemo class. Yes, I guess there is such a thing.

Penny will have a port installed in her chest to accommodate the IV drips. I am guessing the port will be in there until this is done.

Just another day, and another week in our house. One day, one step at a time. Until we are cancer-free.

CHAPTER 9: THE FIRST DAY OF CHEMO TREATMENT

"Love cures people..." - Karl Menninger

◆ ◆ ◆

Summer is passing and it is time for the kids to start back to school. On the first day of class, we settled each of our children into their new elementary classroom with their new teacher. At each stop I pulled the teacher aside, introduced myself, and shared that that our family was in the middle of a journey taking on breast cancer. I wanted each teacher to be observant of any signs of our kids being impacted from things at home, and to keep us informed. I think our kids have been resilient so far. There could be a chance that they surface some feelings in school as the journey continues.

This is also the week that Penny starts her chemo treatments. The treatments will consist of three IV drips – Taxotere, Carboplatin, and Herceptin once every three weeks for the next eighteen weeks, ending around Christmas. The Carboplatin is the chemo drug. Each treatment will last for three to four hours. This will be the phase where Penny will take on side effects of nausea, fatigue and hair loss.

We sat in a chemo class last week. It is a small world when

you know someone in the class. Cancer is everywhere. I am more aware of it. From TV to real life, it feels like cancer is there. Andrea Mitchell of NBC announced this week that she has breast cancer. Amy Roback of Good Morning America, as well as Ann Curry battled breast cancer. A friend at work was diagnosed around the same time as Penny. Another friend at work is a survivor. Yet another reported his Uncle is towards the end of breast cancer treatments. Yes, rare but men can get breast cancer too. Family members, friends from our kid's school, celebrities – breast cancer and cancer, in general, feels everywhere. Andrea Mitchell reported the odds are that one in eight women will be diagnosed with breast cancer. We are not unique in this journey.

Penny is keeping the faith through all this. I know she hurts. Physically she is dealing with the stretchers under the muscle in her chest as part of the reconstruction. She describes it as constant outward pressure from the chest. She had her first saline fill last week, one of many to come over the months ahead. They continue to stretch her chest skin a little at a time. As soon as the pain gets bearable, the cycle begins again.

She also had an IV port placed in her chest yesterday for the IV treatments. The nurse reported that the recovery pain from the day surgery to place in the port should only last four days. Then we will see if the chemo nurse was right in predicting that seven days after chemo fatigue should be worse. As soon as she readjusts to that, she will start to experience hair loss – expected to show signs in seventeen days. Penny is like a boxer in the ring taking painful blows from all directions. As soon as she gets a footing, the next painful blow arrives for her to take on.

Beyond the physical pain, I know it is the mental pain that hurts the most. She is putting on a strong, brave face. I have a front row seat watching her through this whole process. We shared late-night conversations on how she is feeling. Cancer is scary – no one wants it. Physically it consumes the body. But mentally it tortures the mind and soul as well. All the survivors I have talked with report that the mental battle is usually the hardest pain to manage.

My wife reads all the cards, e-mails, Facebook posts from well-wishers. She is appreciative of all the acts of kindness she has received – big and small. They do make a difference. It is nice to know others care. Our family is very appreciative of the wonderful support we have received from all directions. We know our destination. There is just more twist in the road ahead and some more painful blows to take-on to get to where we want to go. Penny is staying strong.

I am afraid too. Sometimes it shows even in the way I stare at Penny for too long. I am in a place far away, a time when there was no cancer in our lives and all we had to mark the calendar with were family vacations and not long hospital visits. I assume and hope everything will be okay, but what if I am wrong?

Cancer had also bonded us in a different way we never thought was possible. In a way, cancer had served as a bridge to greater levels of relationship between us. If we can get through this, I believe we should be able to tackle anything life throws our way. I try to find the positive aspects of this journey to make my mind feel better.

I must assume that in the future after all this, I will come home to a healthy wife and an atmosphere of peace and hope and so many dreams for the future. We are in this together – us against breast cancer.

CHAPTER 10: CHEMO TAKES A PUNCH LANDING US BACK IN THE HOSPITAL

There is a story about two frogs travelling through a forest. Suddenly they both fall into a pit and are trapped. The first frog tries to make his way out of the slippery pit but try as he might; he is unable to get out. Soon the other joins him and together, their pitiful cries draw the attention of some other group of frogs. These ones come to see the two trapped frogs struggling to get out and discourage them.

"Just give up, you will never make it alive," one old frog says."We have been in this forest for too long, nobody has been able to get out alive," an even older frog croaks.

"Maybe things will change tonight," a young toad whispers. "Maybe these ones will change the narrative."

Soon he begins to cheer the two frogs caught in the pit and fueled by the encouragement; they begin to jump harder and harder until poof! They shoot up and out of that pit of misery.

◆ ◆ ◆

Penny had a tough day on Friday. She was feeling extra yucky all day with flu-like symptoms - achy, chills, and generally uncomfortable. When we checked her temperature at 6pm she was 103.5 degrees. That is not what we want to see.

During chemo class, we were instructed to call any time of the day if we ever see a temperature spike above 100. As instructed, we called the oncologist's office and got the answering service and waited for the doctor on call to ring us back. He did and suggested in a calm reassuring voice that we go into the hospital emergency room.

They got Penny admitted right away and ran a battery of tests on her. Her fever was high, her heart rate was high, and her red and white blood count levels were low. Hemoglobin (Red) at 6, when they like to see above 11-12. Neutrophils (White) at 100, when they like to see over 500. Neutrophil granulocytes are the most abundant type of white blood cells.

Basically, Penny's immune system was being suppressed due to the chemo. When the immune system gets suppressed, it is harder for the body to fight off infections and diseases. Penny got a bug in her system that her body could not naturally fight off. They admitted her into the hospital and put her into an isolation room. It is a specially pressurized room that reduces the chance of infections from germs. Nurses and visitors need to put on gloves, mask, and gowns to enter the room. They keep visitors to a minimum.

They think Penny will be in the hospital until at least Monday.

This setback sucks. I am tired of seeing Penny become a member of the Abbott frequent guest program. Don't get me wrong, Abbott is state of the art and the staff is great. Penny is in great hands and being there is a good thing. She is being well cared for. I guess I am just weary from this fight. I am tired of sitting in hospital rooms looking at my wife fighting off pain. I am tired of watching my wife fight off tears. I am tired of feeling helpless knowing the only thing I can do is be there for her. I desperately want to take the pain away from her. I so want this experience to be over.

There are moments of confusion and distraction. A few days after being in isolation a woman we didn't know peered through the window of the door to Penny's room. She gestured for approval before she entered the room in mask and gown. When she greeted us, she stated, "hi, I am Sara from hospice." Hospice! Either someone didn't tell us something, or she was in the wrong room. Much to Sara's horror, she was in the wrong room. For us it ends up being good news and something to briefly take our mind off our situation.

Rationally I know this whole thing will pass. I know we will get through all this. We will gain our strength. Things will be okay. We will rise to the moment. We will win the fight. There will be better days ahead after we get through chemo at the end of the year. Our lives will someday get back closer to normal.

Penny and I will celebrate our twelfth wedding anniversary on September 18th. It looks like we will have an extra special anniversary this year. We will have a private room in a fancy type hotel, called Abbott Hospital. We will enjoy dinner out at the Abbott cafeteria, flowers (just received some more that were delivered today), maybe take in a movie (DVD player in the hospital room). It doesn't come any better than that. That said, this is a deeper and more meaningful anniversary for us. This situation has further deepened my love for my wife. It has also made me realize that when life's challenges come, I have a great partner next to me.

My mind wonders more of late. When I am driving, and at stoplights, I get reflective. I sometimes think about all this and feel a little teary. I remind myself that we will get through all this. One day, one step at a time and before we know it, we will be out of this tunnel. We just need to rise to the moment – take on the immediate challenge in front of us – do the right things – make good decisions - and keep the faith. So, I will.

Like the two frogs, I feel a renewed sense of encouragement inside me and I silently pledge my support to my wife. For better or for worse, in sickness and in health this is a fight I will see to the finish.

CHAPTER 11: HAIR TODAY, GONE TOMORROW

"Nothing makes a woman more beautiful than the belief that she is beautiful." - Sophia Loren

◆ ◆ ◆

I had a dream that all of Penny's hair was gone. It had fallen off while she slept next to me. My hands shook as I reached for a handful of those luxurious locks. I woke up and I wanted to shout for joy, but Penny was sleeping beside me as usual. Then the realization hit me; although this was a dream, it was soon to become my reality. We are at day seventeen after the first chemo treatment. This is around the time when cancer patients begin to lose hair and Penny is no exception. She had earlier reported that a few clumps had come loose yesterday while she was getting prepared for the trip to the hospital.

It is all so bizarre.

After the chemotherapy comes the consequences of having chemicals course through your system consistently. Although the joy that comes from a future that is cancer-free is nothing compared to suffering hair loss, it is nevertheless a period that is approached with trepidation.

Like a scene from a horror movie, we would wake up and the hair will be on the pillow, lying there so innocently like it was never pinned to the scalp from which it has finally pulled away. Although Penny and I had prepared the kids for this phase of her recovery, I doubt if we ourselves were ready for what was to come.

In an act of love and trying to control an uncontrollable situation, I thought it would be positive if we gathered in the backyard as a family and shaved mom's head. I wanted the kids to be part of the process to be less shocked by mom's different look. I set up a chair and clippers in the back yard, alongside a bonfire. I tried to create a celebratory atmosphere. It was hard for Penny to feel celebratory. As I took the electric clipper to her hair, she couldn't contain her emotions and tears. As soon as she started getting emotional, that made me feel emotional and tear up. And soon the kids were all trying to hold back their tears. What a disaster. I probably seared in a devastating memory into my kids' heads. After a little time for Penny to gather herself, we were able to complete the task and make it feel as normal as we could.

The next day Penny picked up her wig from Revamp Salon. She had already paid for half the cost of the wig as a deposit. When she called back to tell the clerk she wanted to settle upon the remaining due, he had informed her that Penny's mom had secretly paid off the remaining balance due. That act of love from her mom drove Penny to happy tears.

The wig looks cute on Penny. She reports that the wig is hot, scratchy, and uncomfortable on her bald head. That makes sense and is understandable. On Friday night, we indulged in some silly fun family moments. We played around with mom's new wig. Each of us took turns trying on the wig pretending to be as beautiful as mom.

Overall, I think Penny has handled treatment well. Sometimes, she gets bursts of energy. More often she naps feeling fatigue kick in. On the positive side, she is starting to eat a little better which is a healthy sign. Chemo robs the mouth of taste buds making all food taste like cardboard.

The next Chemo treatment is ahead. After the recent episode she had at the hospital, they had decided to skip the next chemo treatment. She will still get her Herceptin dosage and some other IVs, like saline. This is to help her maintain some health so she can attend her brother's wedding on October 10.

CHAPTER 12: BACK TO THE HOSPITAL AGAIN

"The darkest hour is before the dawn." - Thomas Fuller

◆ ◆ ◆

Another month has gone by. A month later, where are we? Well, Penny is back in Abbott hospital. It feels like I am living in the movie "Ground Hog Day." On the advice of her oncologist, I took Penny back to the Abbott's ER yesterday (Saturday 10/29). We are getting very familiar with Abbott hospital. I know the best place to park. I know how to get in after visitor hours. I know the quickest routes from the parking garage to the patient rooms. I know the cafeteria hours. If they had a frequent guest program, I think we'd be at gold status.

Penny and chemo don't seem to get along very well. A week after her first treatment, she landed in the hospital. That trip to the ER was also on a Saturday. I remember it too well.

After that bad reaction, Penny's oncologist allowed her to skip her second chemo treatment for her to be in good health for her brother, Justin's wedding to his bride Amanda. That allowed Penny to be in great physical and mental health for this big life event. She looked beautiful for the wedding. She was happy to attend in good spirits and have a chance to see family and friends.

She also decided to take advantage of her chemo holiday and join her group of five close college girlfriends for a few days in warm Cabo, Mexico. The trip was planned before cancer came into Penny's life. They are all turning 40 this year, and this was their "Big Chill" moment to celebrate deep friendships and life.

Once diagnosed with cancer, Penny informed her friends she was going to miss the Cabo trip. She needed to focus on chemo and all its glory. The last place she wanted to find herself was in a hospital in Mexico. But now with her chemo holiday, Penny was able to re-commit and be on a plane heading to Mexico with her dear friends. They had a low-key special time.

The morning after Penny got home from Mexico; we headed back to the oncology clinic for her second round of chemo. It was a long day of treatment. We got there at 8:30am and left at 4:30pm. That was a week ago Friday.

A chemo clinic is strange place. There is rarely an open chair as demand is overwhelming. You see lots of people with bald heads battling cancer. You hear many heroic stories. You start to recognize staff and return visitors. The dullness of hours sitting in a chair getting IV treatment can be lonely and grueling. Some people enjoy the free snacks, watch TV, read a book, or nap. The most fortunate are the people who have visitors. I always attend treatments. Her friend Jenn stopped by in an act of support. Jenn turned her visit into a picnic. She brought lunch and the wonderful, unique uplifting spirit of Jenn.

The first days after chemo were great, they usually are. Penny was in good health and spirits. But later in the week, she started to feel the effects of the treatment. One of the side effects they prepared her for was bone pain.

She said, "I know what they are talking about now when they say bone pain." It doesn't sound like a pleasant experience. She was clearly starting to get kicked from chemo. She was feeling bone pain, fatigue, fever, chills, and general yuck. She has had it tough.

Friday night at 2:30am, I was woken up from a deep sleep

by the sound of my wife throwing up. It is a distinctive sound that bellows out pain in the still of the quiet night.

Penny's head hung down over the toilet. Tears mixed with sweat and the smell of vomit. Vomit was on the stairs, walls, and floor from not making it to the bathroom in time. I was surprised she had anything to throw up. She hadn't really eaten or drank anything for days.

My mother-in-law who was staying with us again to help, was already there by her daughter's side. Jane quickly worked to clean-up the scene and provided aid and comfort to her daughter. As a parent, it is hard to witness your child in pain. Jane is a great mother and person.

It was not a comfortable night for Penny. After seeing no progress, we called the oncologist office, and they suggested we go to the ER, yet again. We got into a private ER room early Saturday. They worked to get Penny comfortable. I found myself in a familiar uncomfortable setting; sitting by Penny in a dimly lit ER room for hours and hours and hours.

I remember sitting in that warm, quiet, dimly lit, cramped ER patient room (number 10 – last visit was room number 7) and watching Penny sleep. I could hear the sound from a humming whoosh of the air vent and an occasional chirping of a machine going off outside Penny's ER room. Penny was resting comfortably. Sleeping was a more comfortable time than when she was awake. She was tired after the lack of sleep from the past few days and nights. Any sleep was welcome. When she was asleep, she couldn't feel her pain. As I watched her, I could see her eyelids fluttering and mouth twitching. I assume Penny was in a deep REM-sleep. I wonder what she dreams about these days.

To pass the time for entertainment I tried to listen to the faint words of interesting conversations outside in the hallway. There are many interesting people visiting the ER. The hospital emergency room is a sad place filled with lots of people with lots of sad stories. Everyday more pain walks through the ER doors.

God bless caregivers.

I sat there with my thoughts. They slipped negative. I wondered if I am watching something worse happening before my eyes. She will get better, right? She will. It is not fun to sit by while someone you love is feeling like shit. Excuse my choice of words – but any others don't seem to capture the feeling as well.

I sat there looking at my wife lying on the hospital gurney looking beautiful with no hair. Her eyes looked droopy from the weight of pain and tears. She looked emaciated to me. I can see her bones through her skin. She has lost more weight. I guess that happens when you don't eat or drink anything and then throw up the little you consume. She woke up and threw up again in the ER. They decided to (re)admit her for another overnight hospital stay. Her new hospital room is right next to the old hospital room she was in after her double mastectomy. I know that area of the hospital and the nurses well.

It's Halloween tomorrow. That means only two more months of this scary time in our life. We have been on this journey since July – four months of this crap. Only two more to go before the hardest part is supposedly over. I am not sure how this consistent bad reaction to chemo that always seems to end in hospital stays will impact Penny's future treatment. Penny can't keep going at this pace if this is how every chemo treatment will feel. They told us it wouldn't be this bad.

Mixed in with get well cards in our mailbox are numerous statements and invoices from doctors, hospitals, pharmacies and clinics. It took me a few hours the other day to sort the mail and figure out who should get paid what. The bills seem more complicated than they should be. I estimate the cost of Penny's care will tally past $100k by the time we are done. I guess it is the cost of living. I guess it is the cost of quality care. Thank God for my health insurance. I couldn't imagine what long-term impact this would have on our family if I didn't have a good job and good insurance. I don't think anyone should have to go into bankruptcy to live.

Penny is improving as the days of her latest hospital stay go by. Each new day is a better day than the past week. Penny is enjoying her hospital care and much-needed IV fluids. She is looking and feeling much better. She is comfortable again and her good spirit is back. We will get her back to good health and get her back home. This too shall pass.

The original plan remains. We will take this one day, one step at a time. We will push on. We will stay strong. We will get through all this and find our way back to our "normal" life.

We continue to receive a lot of support on our doorstep. The support has made the difference. I have told many people that as bad as this whole thing has been, at the same time it has been a special blessing to be able to feel the outpouring of love and support from our great community, family, and friends. For that, I am thankful.

CHAPTER 13: GETTING TO THE END OF THE JOURNEY WITH APPRECIATION

"No duty is more urgent than that of returning thanks." -James Allen

◆ ◆ ◆

It is New Year's Eve and 2011 is a year that I will never forget. It has changed our lives in many ways. It has also changed my view of people and my outlook of the future ahead.

Penny received her last chemo treatment the Thursday before Christmas. The last one has not been easy. The side effects from months of chemo have built up. She is pushing through and working hard to get better every day. The hardest days of our journey will soon be behind us. Penny will continue trips to the Oncology clinic for the next six months to receive Herceptin drips every three weeks. Thankfully, there are no side effects from Herceptin. We expect Penny to start to grow hair back and return to a more normal healthy life.

We look forward to spending many happy years ahead as a family.

As challenging as the past six months has been for Penny and our family, it has been a blessing to be able to feel the power of love and care from community, family, and friends. It has been wonderfully overwhelming and has been a very special experience that will forever change our lives.

We have been blessed to be encircled by good, thoughtful and caring people. I am happy to report that there are many angels in the army of goodness. I have seen them and felt their spirits firsthand. It is good to know when times get tough; great people are there to support us.

Over the past six months... Various family members arrived from Maine, Massachusetts, and Iowa to visit and help.

Numerous people mailed and dropped off meals, salads, sweets, cupcakes, cookies, donuts, bread, and even a few edible fruit arrangements. Our freezer was filled by fellow parents of twins with "Let's Dish Meals." Our home was even stocked with some beer and wine. There were more people wanting to provide a meal, then our calendar could allow. We received many beautiful plants and flower arrangements that brightened Penny's hospital room and our home.

We also received a constant stream of good thoughts and prayers. We received hundreds and hundreds of thoughtful Facebook posts. Daily, the postman delivered thoughtful cards and notes cheering Penny and our family on towards better days. One of Penny's closest childhood friends, Jessica sent a card every week filled with a message of support and cheer. I got a few from her as well.

Our kids received special gift boxes filled with activities, stickers, and CDs. Another of Penny's childhood friends, Amy sent each of our children special "build-a-bears" in nurse outfits, custom inscribed with their names. It was so touching.

We received numerous gift certificates for meals, spa pampering, and even house cleaning services. The folks at Distinctive Cleaning provided some free cleanings. Friends and neighbors offered to babysit of our children and went out of their way to arrange extra play dates to give Penny some quiet time to rest.

We've also had an endless supply of books, magazines, and journals.

Penny received bandanas, shirts, and a very comfy cashmere robe. The Chair hair salon donated services to cut Penny's hair short. Penny's mom purchased part of a beautiful wig. Fellow survivor friends lent the traveling breast cancer club healing reclining chair. Friends walked and raced in Penny's honor during the Susan Komen Race for the Cure. Maine friends decorated tee-shirts for Penny. Friends at Performance Marketing decorated Converse sneakers with messages of hope and strength.

As if all that was not enough... the generous human spirit noted above was heavily punctuated by a card we received last week from Richman's Café in Bellevue Iowa. The card read,

"Everyone at Richman's Café wishes you and your family a Merry Christmas and a Happy and Healthy New Year. We didn't do an exchange of gifts this year. We decided to give... not receive... and you came to mind... we want you to know we will continue to keep you in our thoughts and prayers daily. Keep your faith strong."

The package also included a generous gift. The gesture and hearts of the people from Richman's Café in Bellevue, Iowa are bigger than the size of the gift.

All the outpouring of love and support has been overwhelming and at times hard to receive. Collectively, everyone set a wonderful standard for us to live up to as we payback by paying it forward in life. The healing power of everyone's spirit has provided us everything medicine can't provide. Our belief in the decency and goodness of people has been refortified.

POSTSCRIPT: CANCER FREE!

"We may encounter many defeats, but we must not be defeated." – Maya Angelou

◆ ◆ ◆

As I reflect,

It has been an interesting journey in our lives that has changed us as people. I am happy to report that Penny is in great shape with a fantastic prognosis. We had a meeting with her oncologist who indicated Penny is a success case. She is cancer free and has a 92% lifetime probability of never having to deal with cancer again related to this case.

A great outcome. We arrived taking it one day at a time - us against breast cancer.

Made in the USA
Las Vegas, NV
21 October 2020